NOVA SCOTIA

HARRY BECKETT

Weigl

CALGARY

www.weigl.com

Published by Weigl Educational Publishers Limited
6325 – 10 Street SE
Calgary, Alberta
Canada T2H 2Z9
Web site: http://www.weigl.com

Canadian Cataloguing in Publication Data
Beckett, Harry, 1936
 Nova Scotia

 (Eye on Canada)
 Includes Index
 ISBN 1-896990-87-8

 1. Nova Scotia--Juvenile literature. I. Title. II. Series:
FC2311.2.B43 2000   j971.5   C00-911108-5
F1037.4.B43 2000

Printed and bound in the United States
 2 3 4 5 6 7 8 9 0   05 04

We acknowledge the
financial support of
the Government of
Canada through the
Book Publishing
Industry Development
Program (BPIDP) for
our publishing activities.

Photograph Credits
Every reasonable effort has been made to trace ownership and to obtain
permission to reprint copyright material. The publishers would be pleased to
have any errors or omissions brought to their attention so that they may be
corrected in subsequent printings.

Art Gallery of Ontario: page 18T-R (C.W. Jefferys "The Founding of Halifax, 1749"
purchase 1930 #1688); Art Gallery of Nova Scotia – Collection of Robert and Betty
Flinn, Halifax, Nova Scotia: page 25B; Barrett and MacKay: pages cover, 3M-R, 4T-R,
4B, 5M-L, 5B, 6, 8, 10T-L, 10T-R, 12T-R, 13B, 15B, 20B-L; Bob Semple: page 9B-R;
Black Cultural Center for Nova Scotia: page 23T-L; Canadian Museum of Civilization:
page 16T-L (Oracle series - Bark canoes); Canadian Tourism Commission: pages
3B-R, 7, 9M-L, 12B-L, 12B-R, 14M, 19T-L, 20B-R, 21B, 22, 25T-L, 26B, 27;
Corel Corporation: pages 10M, 11T-L, 11B-L, 14B; Dalhousie University: page 15M;
Federation Acadienne de la Nouvelle-Ecosse: page 23B; Nova Scotia Department of
Agriculture and Marketing: page 10B-R; Men of the Deeps: 24M-R; National Archives
of Canada: pages 17M-L (C-098232), 21M-L (PA-028035); National Gallery of Canada,
Ottawa: pages 3T-R, 16B-L (6663); Nettwerk Management: page 24B; Nova Scotia
Communications –Nova Scotia Creative Services: pages 1, 9T-L; Nova Scotia Fisheries
and Aquaculture: page 13M; Nova Scotia International Tattoo: page 27T-L; Rogers
Communications Inc: pages 17T, 19B; Royal Ontario Museum: page 18B-R (R. Paton
"Louisbourg" ROM 951.1.97); Shubenacadie Tidal Bore Rafting Park Ltd.: page 26T-
R; Universite de Moncton: page 18T-L ("La Dispersion des Acadiens", by Henri Beau.
Collection Musee Acadien).

Project Coordinator
Jill Foran
Design
Lucinda Cage
Warren Clark
Copy Editor
Heather Kissock
Layout
Lucinda Cage
Cover Design
Terry Paulhus
Photo Researcher
Alan Tong

CONTENTS

Introduction 4

Land and Climate 8

Natural Resources 9

Plants and Animals 10

Tourism 12

Industry 13

Goods and Services 14

First Nations 16

Explorers 17

Early Settlers 18

Population 20

Politics and Government 21

Cultural Groups 22

Arts and Entertainment 24

Sports 26

Eye on Canada 28

Brain Teasers 30

More Information 31

Index 32

INTRODUCTION

Nova Scotia is the second smallest province in Canada. It lies on the east coast, and nowhere in the province is more than an hour's drive to the sea. Nova Scotia, New Brunswick, and Prince Edward Island are Canada's **Maritime Provinces**.

Nova Scotia is a **peninsula**. The province is almost entirely surrounded by water. Only a narrow strip of land joins Nova Scotia to the rest of mainland Canada. This strip of land is called the Chignecto Isthmus, and it links the province to its western neighbour, New Brunswick. Nova Scotia and New Brunswick lie opposite each other across the Bay of Fundy. The Northumberland Strait is to the north, between Nova Scotia and Prince Edward Island. The northern part of Nova Scotia, called Cape Breton Island, is separated from the rest of the province by the Strait of Canso. It can only be reached by a road over a narrow **causeway**. At the northeastern end of Cape Breton Island, the Cabot Strait lies between the province and Newfoundland. Nova Scotia's southeast coast faces out to the Atlantic Ocean.

Nova Scotia has a strong sea-faring heritage. Many people in the province live in small fishing villages.

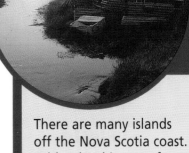

People heading to Nova Scotia can get there by sea, land, or air. The Halifax International Airport is the seventh busiest airport in Canada, with direct flights from New York, Boston, Toronto, Montreal, St. John's, and Houston. There are also smaller airports at Yarmouth and Sydney.

Railways are another way to get to Nova Scotia. Via Rail operates weekly passenger services from Montreal, and container rail service to Halifax from Montreal, Toronto, and Chicago. Privately owned passenger trains run between Truro and Sydney and between Halifax and Kentville.

The sea has always served Nova Scotia as a transportation highway. Ferries run between Digby, Nova Scotia and Saint John, New Brunswick. Another ferry runs between North Sydney, Nova Scotia and Port aux Basques, Newfoundland. Visitors from the United States can take a ferry from Portland or Bar Harbor, which are both in the nearby state of Maine.

Nova Scotia's provincial motto is *Munit haec et altera vincit* which means "One defends and the other conquers."

Drivers can reach Nova Scotia via the Trans-Canada Highway.

Halifax has an advantage over American east coast ports because it is always ice-free. It is also a day's sailing time closer to Europe.

The CAT is North America's fastest car ferry. It runs between Bar Harbour and Yarmouth.

LOCATION MAP

250 km

N
W E
S

Sydney
Louisbourg

Antigonish

Truro Dartmouth
Halifax

Lunenburg

NOVA SCOTIA

Yarmouth

The city of Halifax is the transportation hub of Atlantic Canada.

Nova Scotia is Latin for "New Scotland." The province was named by a Scottish nobleman who saw its distinct similarity to his homeland. Cape Breton's highland landscape looks very much like the highlands of Scotland. Highlands, along with lush forests, wide fields, sparkling lakes, rushing rivers, and rugged coastlines, all contribute to Nova Scotia's picture-perfect scenery.

Nova Scotia's culture is as rich as its scenery. Scottish heritage is evident throughout the province. Mi'kmaq, Acadian, and German communities are also present. Each of these communities adds to the province's diverse identity and festive atmosphere.

Lunenburg is home to a strong German community.

Cape Breton Highlands National Park encompasses 950 sq km of beautiful highland and coastal habitats.

QUICK FACTS

There are more than three thousand lakes in Nova Scotia. The largest is the salt water Bras d'Or Lake.

The Bay of Fundy, which lies between Nova Scotia and New Brunswick, has the highest tides on Earth. Twice a day, more than 100 billion tonnes of sea water rush in and out of the bay, often creating a rise and fall of up to about 3.5 m.

Most of Nova Scotia's rivers are less than 80 km long. The Mersey and the St. Mary's are the longest rivers in the province.

The Annapolis and Shubenacadie rivers flow into the Bay of Fundy.

The Fundy tides are so powerful that they sometimes erode the quartz rocks along the shore of Partridge Island.

Nova Scotia's provincial flower is the mayflower.

In the late 1800s, many Nova Scotians wanted to withdraw from Confederation. On Canada Day they would hang black crepe on their buildings to show they were in mourning.

Nova Scotia has a long and fascinating history. Its past is marked by a number of battles between France and Britain for control of the region. These battles came to an end when Britain seized France's Fort Louisbourg in 1758. Fortresses, monuments, old homes and buildings, and many museums around Nova Scotia serve as landmarks to the province's history.

Nova Scotia was also among the first Canadian provinces. In 1867, Nova Scotia, New Brunswick, Quebec, and Ontario formed the Dominion of Canada.

Historical buildings and landmarks, like this 1832 meeting house, are found all over the province.

At the Fortress Louisbourg National Historic Site, interpreters dress up in period costumes and act out the daily lives of historic townspeople and soldiers.

LAND AND CLIMATE

Nova Scotia is made up of rugged highlands, rolling valleys, and a large number of rivers, lakes, and streams. Two kinds of terrain dominate the province. The Atlantic Upland consists of small mountains with thick forests. It covers most of Nova Scotia. Lowlands lie between the uplands. These valley regions are carved out by erosion, caused by wind and water. The major lowland is the Annapolis Valley.

The weather in Nova Scotia challenges **meteorologists**. Nova Scotia lies between two strong ocean currents: the cold Labrador Current, which comes from the Arctic Ocean, and the warm Gulf Stream, which comes from the Gulf of Mexico. The mixing of these two currents results in Nova Scotia's moderate winters and cool summers. It also plays a key role in producing thick sea fogs.

Nova Scotia's northern highlands consist of rocks that are about 400 million years old.

NATURAL RESOURCES

Water is Nova Scotia's most important resource. The province has many rivers and lakes which provide Nova Scotians with a huge supply of fresh water, **hydroelectric power**, and transportation routes for the mining and logging industries. The sea provides **ground fish** such as haddock and cod, and shellfish such as scallops and lobsters. Fishing is an essential part of Nova Scotia's economy.

Most of the province was once covered in forests. Today, forests cover about 75 percent of the land, but many of these forests are secondary growth **coniferous** forests. This means they are made up of new trees that were planted to replace ones cut down. Nova Scotia's trees have served the lumber industry well.

The main mineral resource in Nova Scotia is coal. There are also deposits of salt and construction minerals such as sand, gypsum, and gravel in the province.

In May 1992, twenty-six men were killed in the Westray Mine disaster. In 1998, the remainder of the mine was destroyed.

Recent discoveries of gas and oil around Sable Island have added to the province's economy.

The soil in Nova Scotia is thin, stony, and not very fertile, except in the Annapolis Valley and along the Northumberland coastal plain.

Pugwash is the site of a large salt mine. Each year, the mine produces more than one million tonnes of the world's purest salt.

Lobsters are abundant in Nova Scotia's waters. They are one of the province's most valuable catches.

PLANTS AND ANIMALS

The fall season brings beautiful colours to Nova Scotia's landscapes.

Nova Scotia's plant life is surprisingly diverse, considering the small size of the province.

The northern half of Cape Breton Island is part of the vast coniferous forest that covers most of northern Canada. Trees there include white spruce and balsam fir.

To the south, there are mostly spruce, tamarack, hemlock, pine, and fir mixed with some **deciduous** trees such as maple, birch, beech, and ash. Bushes such as clintonia, cranberries, and blueberries are everywhere. Wildflowers such as mayflowers, insect-eating pitcher plants, water lilies, and violets grow throughout the province. Mosses, ferns, and lichens grow in the marshy and rocky areas, and a European import, the cuckooflower, has spread through the Annapolis Valley.

The osprey is the provincial bird.

The Nova Scotia Duck Tolling Retriever is the provincial dog.

Sable Island has the largest breeding colony of grey seals and harbour seals in the western Atlantic.

Every summer, 2 million sand pipers gather on the mud of the Bay of Fundy to feed on mud shrimps before starting their non-stop flight to South America.

All kinds of wildlife can be found in Nova Scotia's forests. Large animals such as bears, moose, and deer live there, but smaller animals are more common in the province. Foxes, skunks, porcupines, minks, otters, and weasels are all native to Nova Scotia.

Duck, grouse, pheasant, and bald eagles are among the many birds that frequent the area. Marine life includes cod, swordfish, trout, lobsters, scallops, and oysters. Whales are a common sight around Digby Neck.

Nova Scotia wildlife, like wildlife around the world, is at risk. Because the province burns so much coal to generate electricity, sulphur emissions are a problem. More emissions are carried over the province by westerly winds from the northeastern United States. Precipitation falls through these pollutants and becomes acidic. Eventually, the lakes become acidic and are unable to support wildlife. The Nova Scotia government's main environmental concern is the improvement of water control and the preservation of salmon and trout habitats.

The white-tailed deer is the most common large animal in Nova Scotia.

North American porcupines live mostly in coniferous forests.

TOURISM

Visitors can learn more about Nova Scotia's long and exciting history at many of the province's tourist attractions. Fort Louisbourg on Cape Breton Island was once a seaport and **fortified** town. It was built by the French and destroyed by the British about 250 years ago. The fortress has been rebuilt in accurate detail. Costumed guides in the roles of soldiers, villagers, and noblemen take visitors back to 1744.

The Halifax Citadel National Historic Site is the most visited national site in Canada. Visitors can explore this star-shaped fortress, which was built between 1828 and 1856, and learn more about the naval and military history of Nova Scotia. At the Maritime Museum of the Atlantic, visitors can see exhibits of the Halifax Explosion and artifacts recovered from the *Titanic*, which sank near Halifax in 1912.

Over 100,000 visitors a year follow the Evangeline Trail. This trail goes through the Acadian villages on the Fundy shore to the reconstructed French Habitation at Port Royal, Canada's oldest permanent European settlement.

The Halifax Citadel National Historic Site features a restored library, detention cells, and barrack rooms from the 1800s.

Daily re-enactments of eighteenth century military life take place at many of Nova Scotia's historical sites.

QUICK FACTS

Nova Scotia has more historic sites than any other province except Quebec.

Alexander Graham Bell, a famous inventor, spent his summers in Baddeck. Today, the Alexander Graham Bell National Historic Site contains a museum honouring his life and work.

The Port Royal Habitation National Historic Site brings visitors back to the early seventeenth century, when French explorers first settled in Nova Scotia.

Thousands of people drive the 43 km from Halifax to see the famous harbour and lighthouse at Peggy's Cove.

INDUSTRY

Service and financial industries are important to Nova Scotia. There are more office buildings, schools, and hotels in the province than there are factories.

Nova Scotia is known for its prominent fishing industry. Cod, haddock, herring, lobster, and scallops are among the fish that contribute to the province's economy. Most of Nova Scotia's farmland is in the Annapolis Valley and in northern parts of the province. The province is best known for growing fruits and vegetables, but dairy farming is the largest agricultural sector.

Manufacturing is also an important industry. Iron and steel manufacturing, food processing, and paper production are among the most important manufacturing activities. Most of these small plants process local products such as fish, fruit, livestock, and pulpwood.

The first commercial use of Nova Scotia's trees was for shipbuilding.

The provincial government employs large numbers of people in its Halifax departments and its regional offices.

Nova Scotia is second to British Columbia in the value of its fisheries.

Pictou is one of the largest live lobster harvesting ports in the world.

Nova Scotia is an important supplier of Christmas trees. Every year, thousands of evergreens are exported from the province to other markets.

More than two dozen kinds of marine life are harvested in Nova Scotia's waters.

The Annapolis Valley is known for its delicious apple harvests. Most of the apple orchards are family owned.

GOODS AND SERVICES

Nova Scotia has an extensive network of roads, railways, and maritime shipping routes. The harbour at Halifax remains ice-free year round and has excellent facilities for ocean-going vessels. It is second only to Montreal in the number of ships that visit.

There are more than 750 km of rail lines in the province, many of which are used for shipping goods to other parts of Canada. One of Nova Scotia's most important traffic routes is the Canso Causeway. It links mainland Nova Scotia to Cape Breton Island, and it carries both highway and railway traffic. The creation of the causeway made heavy industry possible in Cape Breton. Nova Scotia also has a good roadway system. As the province is so far away from the large markets of Central Canada, improvements to the roads are always a priority.

The Canso Causeway was completed in 1955. It enables cars and trains to carry goods to and from Cape Breton.

The Halifax harbour is Canada's busiest east coast port. It also serves as Canada's main naval base.

Nova Scotia Community College has eighteen campuses around the province.

The Gaelic College of Celtic Arts and Crafts is the only one of its kind in North America.

The Bedford Institute of Oceanography, in Dartmouth, is one of Canada's largest facilities for conducting research in marine sciences.

Nova Scotia's main medical research facility is the Faculty of Medicine at Dalhousie University.

The Bank of Nova Scotia is one of the largest banks in Canada.

About two-thirds of Nova Scotia's work force are employed in service industries such as transportation, public administration, power generation, finance, retail sales, and health and education.

The province has many degree-granting colleges and universities. Dalhousie University is the largest and most well-known of the schools in Nova Scotia. A lesser known college is the **Gaelic** College of **Celtic** Arts and Crafts. This unique school is located on Cape Breton Island and is dedicated to the preservation of Celtic and Gaelic culture in Nova Scotia. It holds courses in the Gaelic language and offers instruction in such things as Highland dancing, bagpiping, and fiddling.

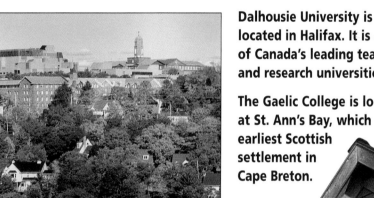

Dalhousie University is located in Halifax. It is one of Canada's leading teaching and research universities.

The Gaelic College is located at St. Ann's Bay, which is the earliest Scottish settlement in Cape Breton.

FIRST NATIONS

For centuries before European explorers arrived, thousands of **nomadic** Mi'kmaq lived in the Nova Scotia region. The first Europeans they met were probably Vikings.

The waters and woods in the Nova Scotia region were rich in fish and wildlife and the Mi'kmaq lived mostly by hunting and fishing. They would live near the seashore in the summer, where they could easily catch fish. In the winter, they would move into the woods where they would hunt for wildlife and take shelter from the cold.

The Mi'kmaq were skilled at fishing and hunting. Fishing was often done at night from canoes. The Mi'kmaq carried birchbark torches and speared the fish that were attracted by the light. They also used lit torches to surprise and attract birds. Hunting large animals was reserved for the winter, when snow made it harder for the animals to escape.

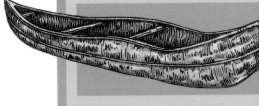

In the early 1500s, the Mi'kmaq traded goods with European fishers who came to Canada every year. Furs would be traded for goods such as guns and beads.

EXPLORERS

A stone with **runic** writing on it was found in 1812 near Yarmouth. The fact that the Vikings used this form of writing suggests that they may have explored the area long ago.

Although both Britain and France claimed the land in the Nova Scotia region, neither nation was interested in settlement. The English were interested in the fur trade and the French in the fisheries.

The people at Port Royal founded the "Order of Good Cheer," which was dedicated to making each evening's meal a happy and memorable event.

Port Royal was abandoned after two years, re-established in 1610, then destroyed three years later by an English pirate.

The actual spot of John Cabot's 1497 landing is questionable—he and his crew landed either in Labrador, Newfoundland or on Cape Breton.

Viking explorers may have reached Nova Scotia about five centuries before John Cabot arrived on Cape Breton Island in 1497. Cabot claimed the Nova Scotia region for Henry VII of England, then left. Tales that fish could be scooped from the sea in baskets soon brought European fishing boats to the northeast coast. Explorers also came. Jacques Cartier passed through the Cabot Strait in 1534, and claimed the land he saw for King Francis I of France.

It was not until 1605 that Europeans truly began to settle in Nova Scotia. That year, French explorers Pierre de Monts and Samuel de Champlain, along with 125 colonists, arrived on St. Croix Island, which is between New Brunswick and Maine. The next spring, they set up a permanent farming settlement at Port Royal, located on the southwest coast of what is now Nova Scotia. The French named the whole Maritime region Acadia, which was a mythical name meaning "peaceful land."

EARLY SETTLERS

An American poet named Henry Wadsworth Longfellow made Nova Scotia famous in his poem "Evangeline." The poem tells how Acadians were driven from their homes in Nova Scotia by British troops. Today, an area of the province is nicknamed "Land of Evangeline."

Over the next century, there were many battles and disputes between the British and the French over ownership of the Maritime region. In 1713, an agreement called the Treaty of Utrecht gave all of Acadia, except Cape Breton Island and Prince Edward Island, to Britain. The British allowed the Acadians to stay as long as they promised loyalty to Britain. The Acadians refused, but promised instead to remain **neutral** in any struggles between France and Britain.

The British settlement of Nova Scotia began with the founding of Halifax in 1749. Thousands of settlers came from Britain and other parts of Europe, and many more arrived from the British colonies in America. As conflicts with France continued, the British were concerned that the Acadians would side with the French. In an effort to prevent this possibility, the British **expelled** more than 6,000 Acadians and moved them to other colonies in 1755.

The 1758 fall of Louisbourg, which was built to protect the French fishing interests, marked the end of the French colonies in Canada.

The arrival of the Loyalists doubled the population of Nova Scotia in just one year.

American settlers introduced the importance of town meetings and elections to Nova Scotians.

In 1784, Nova Scotia, New Brunswick, and Cape Breton Island were made into separate colonies. Cape Breton Island was reunited with Nova Scotia in 1820.

Between 1815 and 1838, about 20,000 Scottish people and many Irish people came to Canada. A large number chose Nova Scotia as their home.

Nova Scotia's population continued to increase. Britain offered free land to potential settlers in order to attract people to the region. More immigrants from Scotland, Ireland, and England arrived, along with New Englanders. In 1763, the French, through the Treaty of Paris, gave their lands in North America to the British. At this time, many of the deported Acadians returned to the Maritimes and built new settlements.

During the American Revolution (1775-1783), about 30,000 **Loyalists** immigrated to the Nova Scotia region. These people were colonists who wished to remain loyal to Britain, and therefore did not want to stay in the newly independent United States. A large amount of building took place with the many new settlers who came to make their homes in the region. By the mid 1800s, construction of military bases, mining, and farming were all well underway in Nova Scotia.

Nova Scotia's population grew so large with the arrival of the Loyalists that it had to be divided into smaller colonies.

POPULATION

There are just under one million people living in Nova Scotia. The population is distributed quite evenly throughout the province. The Halifax Regional Municipality is the financial, cultural, and commercial centre of Nova Scotia. With about 355,000 inhabitants, it makes up more than one third of the provincial population.

Nearly 114,000 people live in the second-biggest community, the Cape Breton Regional Municipality, which includes Sydney and Louisbourg. Although always a fishing and fish processing area, it is now developing information technology, machinery, and ocean sciences.

Nova Scotia's heartland community is the town of Truro, which has been an agricultural marketplace for generations. Yarmouth has strong connections with the New England states across the Bay of Fundy because of their common history of fishing and commerce.

QUICK FACTS

Halifax is the biggest city in the Maritimes.

Dartmouth and Halifax are often called twin cities. Dartmouth is situated northeast of Halifax, across the harbour.

In 1996, the cities of Halifax and Dartmouth, along with the rest of Halifax County, were combined to form the Halifax Regional Municipality.

People of British descent make up about 70 percent of Nova Scotia's population.

Acadians make up about 12 percent of Nova Scotia's population.

There are about 11,000 Mi'kmaq in Nova Scotia.

The ferry between Dartmouth and Halifax is a popular way to commute between the cities.

This sign in downtown Halifax points to some of the city's most interesting sites.

POLITICS AND GOVERNMENT

Nova Scotia is governed by a one-chamber legislature with fifty-two members. The majority party forms the government, and its leader is the premier, who appoints a cabinet. The cabinet sets government policy and each minister is responsible for seeing that his or her department carries out these policies.

Below the provincial legislature is the regional, city, town, or rural municipality. The municipal government is responsible for local services but, in the last thirty or forty years, the province has taken over many of these.

Nova Scotia has always had problems with raising money because it is small and not heavily industrialized. It also has a high unemployment rate and must often turn to the federal government for help. Despite economic problems, Nova Scotians remain hopeful and determined to build a more prosperous province.

Nova Scotia is represented federally by eleven members in the House of Commons and nine Senators.

Three prime ministers of Canada have come from Nova Scotia: Sir John Sparrow David Thompson, Sir Charles Tupper, and Sir Robert Borden.

Women in Nova Scotia received the right to vote on April 26, 1918.

Nova Scotia's Legislative Assembly meets at Province House in downtown Halifax. Province House is Canada's oldest Parliament Building.

CULTURAL GROUPS

Perhaps the strongest cultural presence in Nova Scotia is the Scottish culture. People of Scottish descent make up about 25 percent of the province's population. Festivals that celebrate Scottish heritage are held throughout Nova Scotia. The Antigonish Highland Games are among the province's most famous Scottish celebrations. Held every July since 1863, the Highland Games are an excellent demonstration of art, strength, and skill. Athletic competitions, Highland dancing, pipe band competitions, and art displays are all part of the games. Other Scottish festivals include the International Gathering of the Clans in Halifax and the Celtic Colours International Festival, where the sounds of fiddles, pipes, and singing can be heard all over Cape Breton.

Nova Scotians of Scottish descent celebrate their heritage with customs such as bagpiping and Highland dancing.

The Black Cultural Centre, near Dartmouth, celebrates Nova Scotia's African-Canadian heritage with exhibits and special events.

Acadian Rappie Pie, Planked Salmon, Lunenburg Pudding, tangy Solomon Gundy, and Blueberry Grunt are all distinct Nova Scotian dishes.

Lunenburg is made up of a strong German community. There are Oktoberfest celebrations held there every year.

Dutch, Hungarians, and Italians make up small minorities in Nova Scotia.

Nova Scotia celebrates African Heritage Month every February.

Acadians live mostly in northeastern Cape Breton, and many of them continue to speak the Acadian **dialect** of French that was developed long ago. The Acadians in Nova Scotia are proud of their culture, and they share their pride with others through various festivals and fairs. The Grand-Pré National Historic Site was established as a memory to the Acadian settlers who were deported to British colonies. A stone church on the site serves as a museum that exhibits Acadian history. Also, the Acadian Museum in the town of Chéticamp, features French-Canadian antiques, glassware, and rugs.

There is still a relatively large population of Mi'kmaq in Nova Scotia. Most Mi'kmaq live on one of the thirteen reserves in the province, but many others have moved into towns and cities. The Mi'kmaq celebrate their distinct culture at Chapel Island Indian Mission and the Shelburne County Museum, which displays artifacts detailing the area's Mi'kmaq history.

West Pubnico holds an Acadian festival every summer. One of the most popular features of the festival is the Children's Parade.

ARTS AND ENTERTAINMENT

Nova Scotia has a rich tradition of music that ranges from Acadian jigs to Celtic rock. Towns and villages throughout the province are filled with song all year round.

Bagpiping and fiddling contests are a major part of the Antigonish Highland Games. They can also be heard at the Gaelic Mod at St. Ann's and at the International Gathering of the Clans in Halifax.

Many Nova Scotian musicians are appreciated around the world. Anne Murray, from Springhill, has sold more than 20 million albums. Ashley MacIsaac, of Antigonish, entertains listeners with his lively fiddling, and Sarah McLachlan, originally from Halifax, has released several top-selling albums.

Sarah McLachlan studied classical guitar, piano, and voice while growing up in Halifax.

In August, jugglers, musicians, magicians, acrobats, and actors show off their talents at The Halifax International Busker Festival.

Maud Lewis is known as the mother of Nova Scotian folk art.

Every September, Mahone Bay holds the Great Scarecrow Festival and Antique Fair. Scarecrows, square dancing, musicals, fiddling, and craft demonstrations are all part of the fun.

The Chester Playhouse presents concerts, comedies, and dramas to Chester residents and visitors.

There is more to Nova Scotia's arts scene than great music. The province is home to many excellent theatre companies and programs. The Atlantic Theatre Festival runs every summer in Wolfville. The festival presents about three major plays at its Wolfville theatre and occasionally performs in other Nova Scotia areas. Festival Antigonish is another summer theatre celebration. Drama, musicals, comedies, and children's plays are performed throughout July and August. The Neptune Theatre in Halifax presents many lively plays throughout the year.

Visual art that celebrates Maritime culture can be found all over the province. The Art Gallery of Nova Scotia in Halifax displays works of Maritime artists, as well as paintings from around the world. Folk art can be seen throughout the province, especially at Scottish festivals and fairs. Craft festivals attract many visitors every year.

Three Black Cats is just one example of Maud Lewis' cheerful paintings. Thousands of people from Canada and the rest of the world visit the galleries that display her colourful work.

SPORTS

It is commonly thought that hockey was invented by English soldiers who were stationed in Halifax. Stick and ball games were popular in England, and soldiers found these games easy to adapt to Nova Scotia's winter conditions. Later, a puck took the place of the ball because it was easier to control. Several Nova Scotian players, including Al MacInnis, play in the National Hockey League. Jonathan Sim and Colin White, who played together as juniors in New Glasgow, opposed each other in the 1999 Stanley Cup finals. Snowmobiling, cross-country skiing, and curling are other favourite winter sports.

Nova Scotia's sea-faring tradition is still alive in the many residents who sail and windsurf, especially in the warmer waters of the Northumberland Strait. The *Bluenose*, a famous Nova Scotian **schooner,** was victorious many times during the 1920s and 1930s in the International Fisherman's Trophy races.

Rafting is another popular water sport in Nova Scotia. The powerful Fundy tides push against the flow of the river and create waves, called **tidal bores**, that move upstream. Rafting on tidal bores is an exciting summertime activity.

In 1946, the original *Bluenose* ran aground on a coral reef and sank. The *Bluenose II* is an exact replica of the earlier ship. It was built in 1963.

Teams of military personnel from all over the world compete in gun running, hurdles, obstacle courses, and pipe and brass band competitions at the Nova Scotia International Tattoo.

The National Universities Basketball Championships are played annually at the Metro Centre in Halifax.

Experts rate the golf courses of Nova Scotia among the best in the country.

With a quarter of the population being of Scottish descent, Highland Games competitions are popular. The games have athletes running a five-mile road race, throwing a hammer, and tossing the caber. A caber is a peeled log, about 8 m long and 15 cm in diameter, the size of a small telephone pole. Athletes must hold the caber upright in their hands and lean it against their shoulders. Then, they must toss it end over end. The toss requires immense skill and strength.

In the hammer throw, athletes throw a Scottish hammer, which consists of a 7-kg metal ball with a wooden handle attached to it. The athlete must not move his or her feet when the hammer is thrown. The stone throw is another event. The athlete must throw an 11-kg rock, shot-put style, with only one hand. Each contestant gets three throws, but only the longest throw is counted in final scoring.

The Antigonish Highland Games are the longest running Highland Games in North America. They have been held since 1863.

EYE ON CANADA

Nova Scotia is one of the ten provinces and three territories that make up Canada. Compare Nova Scotia's statistics with those of other provinces and territories. What differences and similarities can you find?

Northwest Territories

Entered Confederation:
July 15, 1870

Capital: Yellowknife

Area: 171,918 sq km

Population: 41,606
Rural: 58 percent
Urban: 42 percent

Population Density:
0.24 people per sq km

Yukon

Entered Confederation:
June 13, 1898

Capital: Whitehorse

Area: 483,450 sq km

Population: 30,633
Rural: 40 percent
Urban: 60 percent

Population Density:
0.06 people per sq km

British Columbia

Entered Confederation:
July 20, 1871

Capital: Victoria

Area: 947,800 sq km

Population: 4,023,100
Rural: 18 percent
Urban: 82 percent

Population Density:
4.24 people per sq km

Alberta

Entered Confederation:
September 1, 1905

Capital: Edmonton

Area: 661,190 sq km

Population: 2,964,689
Rural: 20 percent
Urban: 80 percent

Population Density:
4.48 people per sq km

Saskatchewan

Entered Confederation:
September 1, 1905

Capital: Regina

Area: 652,330 sq km

Population: 1,027,780
Rural: 28 percent
Urban: 72 percent

Population Density:
1.57 people per sq km

Manitoba

Entered Confederation:
July 15, 1870

Capital: Winnipeg

Area: 649,950 sq km

Population: 1,143,509
Rural: 28 percent
Urban: 72 percent

Population Density:
1.76 people per sq km

250   500 km

Nunavut

Entered Confederation:
April 1, 1999

Capital: Iqaluit

Area: 1,900,000 sq km

Population: 27,039

Population Density:
0.014 people per sq km

CANADA

Confederation:
July 1, 1867

Capital: Ottawa

Area: 9,203,054 sq km

Population: 30,491,294
Rural: 22 percent
Urban: 78 percent

Population Density:
3.06 people
per sq km

Quebec

Entered Confederation:
July 1, 1867

Capital: Quebec City

Area: 1,540,680 sq km

Population: 7,345,390
Rural: 21 percent
Urban: 79 percent

Population Density:
4.77 people per sq km

Newfoundland & Labrador

Entered Confederation:
March 31, 1949

Capital: St. John's

Area: 405,720 sq km

Population: 541,000
Rural: 43 percent
Urban: 57 percent

Population Density:
1.33 people
per sq km

Prince Edward Island

Entered Confederation:
July 1, 1873

Capital:
Charlottetown

Area: 5,660 sq km

Population: 137,980
Rural: 56 percent
Urban: 44 percent

Population Density:
24.38 people
per sq km

Ontario

Entered Confederation:
July 1, 1867

Capital: Toronto

Area: 1,068,580 sq km

Population: 11,513,808
Rural: 17 percent
Urban: 83 percent

Population Density:
10.77 people per sq km

New Brunswick

Entered Confederation:
July 1, 1867

Capital: Fredericton

Area: 73,440 sq km

Population: 754,969
Rural: 51 percent
Urban: 49 percent

Population Density:
10.28 people per sq km

Nova Scotia

Entered Confederation:
July 1, 1867

Capital: Halifax

Area: 55,490 sq. km

Population: 939,791
Rural: 45 percent
Urban: 55 percent

Population Density:
16.94 people
per sq km

BRAIN TEASERS

Test your knowledge of Nova Scotia by trying to answer these mind-boggling brain teasers!

1 Make a Guess:

What do you call sheep's organs minced with oatmeal, suet, and onions packed in a sheep's stomach and boiled to perfection?

2 Multiple Choice:

The Silver Dart is:

a. a fast-paced train that runs in Nova Scotia.

b. the airplane that took part in the first manned flight in Canada.

c. one of Nova Scotia's many car ferries.

d. a poisonous fish found in Nova Scotia's waters.

3 True or False:

No dinosaur bones have been found in Nova Scotia.

6 Multiple Choice:

A Ceilidh is:

a. a festival of piping, singing, and dancing.

b. a musical instrument.

c. a type of dance.

d. a Scottish costume.

4 Multiple Choice:

What Nova Scotia city was first named Chebucto?

a. Dartmouth
b. Halifax
c. New Glascow
d. Sydney

5 True or False:

The Great Halifax Explosion of 1917 was the biggest man-made explosion until the bombing of Hiroshima during World War II.

7 True or False:

Thomas Chandler Haliburton, a Nova Scotia judge, is said to have coined the phrase "raining cats and dogs."

8 True or False:

There is a herd of wild horses on Sable Island.

8. **True.**

7. **True.** Haliburton was both a respected judge and an acclaimed writer. He came up with many funny phrases to entertain Canadians.

6. **a.** Ceilidh is Gaelic for a festival.

5. **True.** The explosion was caused by two ships colliding. One of the ships was loaded with explosives.

4. **b.** Halifax. Mi'kmaq residents first named the Halifax area Chebucto, which means " the biggest harbour."

3. **False.** Fossilized bones of the world's smallest dinosaur have been found in Parrsboro.

2. **b.** The first manned flight took place in Baddeck.

1. **Haggis.** Nova Scotians of Scottish descent often enjoy this traditional Scottish dish.

GLOSSARY

causeway: a raised road, usually built to cross water or wet ground

Celtic: relating to people of Scottish descent; also linked to people of Irish and Welsh descent

clans: groups of related families that share common ancestors

coniferous: evergreen trees with needles and cones

deciduous: trees or shrubs that shed leaves every year

dialect: a form of speech that is characteristic of a certain region or area

expelled: forced to leave an area

fortified: walls that have been built to strengthen against attack

Gaelic: the language of Scottish highlanders

ground fish: any fish that lives on or near the bottom of the sea

hydroelectric power: the generation of electricity by water power

Loyalists: colonists who remained loyal to Britain during the American Revolution

Maritime Provinces: the east coast provinces of Canada

meteorologist: a person who is trained in the science of weather conditions

neutral: on neither side during a dispute or war

nomadic: a way of life that involves moving from place to place in search of food and water

peninsula: a piece of land that is almost entirely surrounded by water

runic: an ancient type of writing, used especially by ancient Scandinavians

schooner: a ship with two or more masts

tidal bores: high waves

BOOKS

Kessler, Deirdre, and Tom Wilkinson. *This Land The Maritimes*. Ontario: Fitzhenry & Whiteside, 1990.

LeVert, Suzanne. *Nova Scotia*. From *Let's Discover Canada* series. New York: Chelsea House Publishers, 1992.

Thompson, Alexa. *Nova Scotia*. From *Hello Canada* series. Minneapolis: Lerner Publishing Group, 1995.

WEB SITES

Explore Nova Scotia
http://explore.gov.ns.ca

Government of Nova Scotia
http://www.gov.ns.ca

Fort Louisbourg
http://fortress.uccb.ns.ca/

Some Web sites stay current longer than others. To find more information on Nova Scotia, use your Internet search engine to look up such topics as "Nova Scotia," "Halifax," "Maritime Provinces," or any other topic you want to research.

INDEX

Acadia 17, 18
Acadian 6, 12, 18, 19, 20, 23, 24
American Revolution 19, 31
Annapolis Valley 8, 9, 10, 13
Antigonish 5, 24, 25
Antigonish Highland Games 22, 24, 27
Art Gallery of Nova Scotia 25
Atlantic Ocean 4
Atlantic Theatre Festival 25
Atlantic Upland 8

Bay of Fundy 4, 6, 11, 20, 26
Bluenose 26

Cabot, John 17
Cabot Strait 4, 17
Cape Breton 4, 6, 10, 12, 14, 15, 17, 18, 19, 20, 22, 23
Cartier, Jacques 17
Champlain, Samuel de 17
Chignecto Isthmus 4
coal 9, 11, 14

Dalhousie University 15
Dartmouth 5, 15, 20, 23, 30
Digby 5, 11

Evangeline Trail 12

Festival Antigonish 25
fishing 4, 9, 13, 16, 17, 18, 20
forests 6, 8, 9, 11
Fort Louisbourg 7, 12, 31

Halifax 4, 5, 8, 12, 13, 14, 15, 18, 20, 21, 22, 24, 25, 26, 27, 29, 30, 31
Halifax Citadel National Historic Site 12
hockey 26

Loyalists 19, 31
Lunenburg 6, 23, 26

MacIsaac, Ashley 24
McLachlan, Sarah 24
manufacturing 13
mayflowers 7, 10
Mi'kmaq 6, 16, 20, 23, 30
Monts, Pierre, de 17
Murray, Anne 24

Neptune Theatre 25
New Brunswick 4, 5, 6, 7, 17, 19
Newfoundland 4, 5, 17
Northumberland Strait 4, 26

Pictou 13
Port Royal 12, 17

Sable Island 4, 9, 11, 14, 30
Sydney 5, 20, 30

Treaty of Paris 19
Treaty of Utrecht 18
Truro 5, 20

Vikings 16, 17

Wolfville 25

Yarmouth 5, 17, 20

THE WORLD AT WAR
WORLD WAR II

The Home Front

Heinemann Library
Chicago, Illinois

. . . . Brenda Williams

© 2006 Heinemann Library,
a division of Reed Elsevier Inc.
Chicago, Illinois

Customer Service 888-454-2279
Visit our website at www.heinemannlibrary.com

For more information address the publisher:
Heinemann Library, 100 N. LaSalle, Suite 1200,
Chicago, IL 60602

Editorial: Andrew Farrow and Dan Nunn
Design: Lucy Owen and Tokay Interactive Ltd
 (www.tokay.co.uk)
Picture Research: Hannah Taylor and Sally
 Claxton
Production: Duncan Gilbert

Originated by Repro Multi Warna
Printed and bound in China by
 WKT Company Limited

ISBN 0 431 10377 1
10 09 08 07 06
10 9 8 7 6 5 4 3 2 1

**Library of Congress Cataloging-in-
Publication Data**

Williams, Brenda, 1943-
  The home front / Brenda Williams.
    p. cm. -- (World at war-- World War II)
  Includes bibliographical references and index.
  ISBN 1-4034-6194-5 (library binding-hardcover)
  1. World War, 1939-1945--Social aspects.
  2. Social history--20th century.
  3. Social change.
  I. Title. II. Series.
  D744.6.W55 2005
  973.917--dc22
                                2005014763

Acknowledgements
The publishers would like to thank the following
for permission to reproduce photographs:

Australian War Memorial p. **27 top**; Corbis pp. **4**
(Hulton Deutsch Collection), **5** (Bettmann), **6
right** (Bettmann), **8** (Hulton Deutsch Collection),
9 (Hulton Deutsch Collection), **10, 11 bottom**
(Bettmann), **11 top** (Hulton Deutsch Collection),
13 (Bettmann), **14** (Hulton Deutsch Collection),
17 (Hulton Deutsch Collection), **20, 23 bottom**
(Hulton Deutsch Collection), **24** (Hulton Deutsch
Collection), **25** (Hulton Deutsch Collection), **26**
(Bettmann), **27 bottom** (Bettmann), **28**
(Bettmann); Getty Images pp. **15 bottom**
(Hulton Archive), **16** (Hulton Archive), **18
bottom** (Hulton Archive), **19 bottom** (Hulton
Archive), **19 top** (Time Life Pictures), **21** (Hulton
Archive), **22** (Hulton Archive); Imperial War
Museum pp. **7, 23 top**; Topfoto.co.uk pp. **6 left**
(The Lord Price Collection), **12** (LAPI/Roger
Viollet), **15 top** (Roger Viollet), **18 top** (Public
Record Office/HIP).

Cover photograph of a family fitting their
gas masks reproduced with permission of Topham
Picturepoint.

Every effort has been made to contact copyright
holders of any material reproduced in this book.
Any omissions will be rectified in subsequent
printings if notice is given to the publishers.

The paper used to print this book comes from
sustainable resources.

CONTENTS

THE HOME FRONT **4**
The Build-Up to War **6**

LIFE IN WARTIME **8**
Schooling in Wartime **10**

LIVING BEHIND ENEMY LINES **12**
Resistance Fighters **14**

NATIONS HOLD ON **16**
Digging for Victory **18**

MAKE DO WITH LESS **20**
Coping with Rationing **22**

FAMILY LIFE **24**
Keeping in Touch **26**

A CHANGED WORLD **28**

TIMELINE **29**

GLOSSARY **30**

FINDING OUT MORE **31**

INDEX **32**

Some words are shown in bold, **like this**. You can find out what they mean by looking in the glossary.

THE HOME FRONT

In most wars, armies fight along battle fronts, lines where the two sides meet. In World War II (1939–1945) there was also a Home Front, because people in every home in every country at war were affected.

A worldwide war

World War II began in Europe. On September 1, 1939, German armies invaded Poland. Two days later, Great Britain and France, followed by allies such as Australia and Canada, declared war on Germany. On December 7, 1941, Japan attacked the U.S. naval base at Pearl Harbor in Hawaii. This brought the United States into the war.

In this global war, millions of people suffered invasion and **occupation**. This happened to the people of China, Poland, Czechoslovakia, the USSR, Norway, the Netherlands, France, Greece, the Philippines, and many other countries. Their villages and cities became battle zones. Families lost their homes and possessions. Millions of men, women, and children were killed or injured. In some countries, **civilian** deaths far outnumbered military **casualties**.

▼ In World War II, armies supported by airplanes moved quickly across countries. These German troops are pictured advancing through Poland in 1939. As the invaders swept through towns and villages, many civilians were killed or forced to flee.

Britain was not invaded, but its people lived through five years of bombing, known as the **Blitz**. For people in the United States, Canada, and Australia, too, the war brought shortages, fears, and great changes in daily life. The Home Front involved everyone, young and old. As the years passed, and wartime rules became routine, people wondered: how long could it last? And would life ever be the same again?

4

September 1, 1939	September 3, 1939	April–May 1940
German armies invade Poland in a *Blitzkrieg* or "lightning war."	Britain and France go to war with Germany but cannot save Poland.	Germany invades Denmark, Norway, Belgium, the Netherlands, and France. In June, Italy joins the war on the side of Germany.

▲ Bombing from the air added to civilians' misery. These people in London tried to save what they could from the ruins of their wrecked homes.

Estimate of deaths in World War II

Country	Military	Civilians
China	1,300,000	Unknown, up to 20 million?
France	213,000	350,000
Germany	3,500,000	780,000
Japan	1,300,000	672,000
Poland	123,000	5,600,000
Soviet Union	11,000,000	7,000,000
United Kingdom	264,000	93,000
United States	292,000	6,000

An estimated 18 million members of the armed forces from all countries died fighting on land, sea, and in the air. There are no accurate figures for civilians, but it is estimated that twice as many may have died during the war.

June 17, 1940

France stops fighting. Britain and its allies stand alone against Germany.

June 22, 1941

Hitler orders German armies to invade the Soviet Union (Russia).

December 7, 1941

Japanese planes attack the U.S. military base at Pearl Harbor, Hawaii. The United States is at war. Britain and its allies declare war on Japan the following day.

The Build-Up to War

The war was not a surprise to people around the world. **Nazi** leader Adolf Hitler had been building up Germany's armed forces for many years. In 1938, Germany had taken over Austria and much of Czechoslovakia to create a bigger German empire or *Reich*.

Hot news

People followed world news in newspapers and on the radio. In countries such as the United States, Great Britain, and France, governments tried to educate their people about the threat from Germany and Japan.

Preparing for war

Many people in the United States did not want to get involved in the war in Europe. However, the U.S. government supplied Britain and France, and later the Soviet Union, with arms and food. Because of this, German submarines attacked U.S. ships. The U.S. government also believed there could be a war with Japan and that the United States should be able to defend itself. It spent billions of dollars on new equipment. In 1940 it began to draft, or call up, men into its armed forces.

▲ On September 3, 1939, two days after Hitler's attack on Poland, New York's evening papers carried news that France and Britain had declared war on Germany.

◀ Gas masks were issued by governments in case enemy planes dropped poison-gas bombs. No one liked wearing the rubber masks. There were even gas masks for horses!

◄ In many countries, **sandbags** were filled to be used as protection around buildings in case of **air raids**. In the fall of 1939, children were also **evacuated** from London and other British cities to escape the bombing.

Eyewitness

In 1941, 13-year-old Peter Nottage was in Hawaii. "I remember my mother's voice as she pulled me back inside. 'It's on the radio. It's war!'"

Peter saw the attack on Pearl Harbor. At first he thought it was a training exercise. Then a plane exploded and he knew it was war.

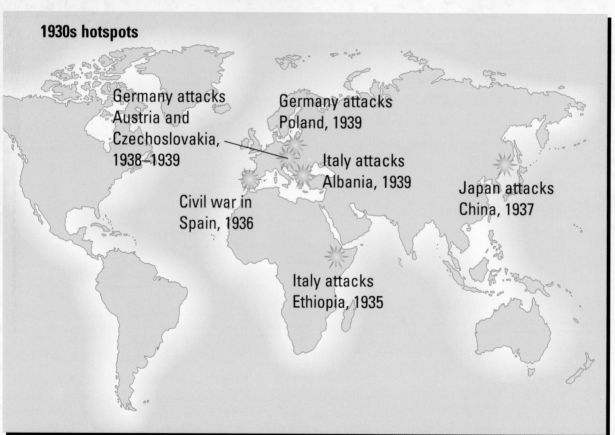

1930s hotspots

Germany attacks Austria and Czechoslovakia, 1938–1939

Germany attacks Poland, 1939

Italy attacks Albania, 1939

Civil war in Spain, 1936

Japan attacks China, 1937

Italy attacks Ethiopia, 1935

▲ In the 1930s, the news media reported on trouble throughout the world. Dictators like Adolf Hitler used military power to get what they wanted. In the 1930s, Germany, Japan, and Italy wanted more territory. Their aggression led the world into war.

LIFE IN WARTIME

During World War II, governments wanted people to live and work as normally as possible. Children went to school, and workers continued to go to their offices and factory jobs. Even when countries like France, Britain, and Germany were bombed, the "war effort" had to go on.

In the United States and Canada, and in most of Australia, daily life went on much like it had before the war. But people had to work harder. Factories were ordered to increase production—more guns, more tanks, more boots, more of everything. People were sent to new jobs in war industries, and some jobs changed— a factory that made wooden furniture, for example, might start making airplanes. Government posters everywhere urged people to work for victory. Radio and newspapers carried war news every day.

Women at work

Millions of women did war work, some going to work for the first time. By January 1944, more than 2.3 million American women had gone to work in the war industry. Yet unfairly, even when doing the same work, women were usually paid less than men. Millions of women combined a job with running a home. Often they were alone because so many men were serving in the military.

▲ A female munitions (weapons) worker in a factory in 1940. Millions of women worked hard to keep factories running and to supply the weapons needed to win the war.

8

May 1940	June 1940	September 1940
In Britain, the working week in aircraft factories increases to 70 hours.	France is defeated. Many French factories begin working for the German war effort.	All American men aged 21–36 must register for possible military service. Women must do the jobs of men who have joined the armed forces.

◀ Streets were often blocked by fallen buildings after an air raid. The ground was strewn with bricks, glass, and shattered wood. Going to work or school often meant a long walk since buses and cars could not get through the debris.

A war for everyone

The war affected everyone, young and old. Most people were **patriotic** and wanted their side to win, but everyone wanted the war to be over. Some people (called conscientious objectors) would not fight for moral reasons. Some were given non-combat posts in the armed forces, some were sent to prison, and many others did Civilian Public Service on farms or in hospitals.

More rules

In wartime there were more rules, less freedom, and shortages of things like metal, tires, and food. Everybody needed ration books to buy food and clothes. But children still had to go to school, even during the **Blitz** (the bombing of British cities).

In the News

In 1942 the U.S. government created the War Production Board. Its job was to allocate vital resources and to oversee war work and production. Its chairman, Donald Nelson, said: "There are a good many ways we can lose this war, but there is only one way to win it. Every man of us must keep his sleeves rolled up [work hard] all the time. Every machine must work all the way around the clock."

9

April–May 1941

The first U.S. ships with essential war food supplies reach Britain.

January 1942

President Roosevelt says that professional baseball should still be played during wartime. It will be good for civilian and military morale.

February 1943

Germany calls up all men and women aged 16–65 for war work.

Schooling in Wartime

LIFE IN WARTIME

The war did not stop education. Most children went to school and took tests, even though many students went directly into the armed forces after they left school. In the United States, more married women became teachers since men were drafted (called up) into the armed forces.

In many countries, schools might be blown up or damaged. Children had to learn to wear gas masks. They hurried to the air raid shelter when the sirens sounded. Inside, safe from the bombs, they listened to stories, sang, or went on with the class until the "all clear" signal.

In some countries, many city children moved to new schools in the countryside, away from bombing. But Jewish children in Nazi-occupied countries were forced to leave their schools. Millions of Jews were sent to concentration camps—prisons holding thousands of captives. Many were killed when they arrived or were worked to death in the camps.

Helping the war effort

Schoolchildren could help the war effort in various ways:

- they collected paper, glass, bones, and scrap metal for recycling

- they saved pocket money to buy **war bonds**

- they saved food scraps to feed to farm animals

- they knitted hats, gloves, and scarves for soldiers and refugees

- they dug "victory gardens" to provide fresh vegetables.

▶ Children in Washington, D.C., collect scrap metal for the war effort.

◀ City children in Great Britain were evacuated to the countryside, away from the bombing. Some schools took over big country houses and summer camps. Country life came as a shock to children who were horrified to see milk coming from "smelly cows," not bottles!

In the News

"The schools and the teachers are in no sense outside the nation's war effort; they are right in it!"
British government leaflet: *The School in Wartime, 1941*

▼ In September 1939, roughly 750,000 British schoolchildren were evacuated. By Christmas, most were settled into new schools. There was another mass evacuation in 1940, after the Blitz on Britain's cities began. It was important to be prepared for air raids: these children are taking shelter under their desks.

Writing letters

Many schoolchildren wrote letters to men and women serving overseas. Jean Barr was a seventh-grade student who wrote to a soldier.

"We wrote to him expressing our appreciation for his military service. Also we included current events taking place in our hometowns."

LIVING BEHIND ENEMY LINES

For millions of people, the war meant living under enemy rule. Every day was a struggle—to find food, to keep warm, to stay alive.

Much of Europe was under Nazi rule from 1940 until 1945. In Asia, the Japanese took over much of China, Southeast Asia, Indonesia, and the Philippines. People in these occupied countries were often treated cruelly, living in fear of imprisonment or death. The occupiers took what they wanted: food, land, houses, farms, factories, even art treasures.

Collaborate or resist?

After France was defeated in 1940, half the country was governed by the Nazis. The other half, known as Vichy, was ruled by French officials who did what the Nazis told them. In France and other occupied countries, some people gave in and decided to help the invaders; they became **collaborators**. Others chose to fight on as members of the "underground" or secret **Resistance** army.

The plight of the Jews

The Nazis had begun to persecute German Jews before the war, and then took this racial hatred across occupied Europe. They rounded up Jews and other peoples, such as Slavs and the Roma (gypsies) from across Poland, the Netherlands, the Soviet Union, and other countries. Some Jewish communities were kept inside walled areas called **ghettos**. This happened in Warsaw, Poland's capital. Many more Jews were taken by train to concentration camps.

▲ Millions of Europeans suffered under Nazi occupation. German soldiers patrolled the streets and stopped to check people's **identity papers**. Anyone suspected of helping the Resistance was shot or hanged.

September 1939	April 9, 1940	May 1940
After the invasion of Poland, Nazis hunt down Jews and force Poles to work for the German war effort.	Germany invades Denmark and Norway. In Norway, Vidkun Quisling heads a government that supports Germany, but most Norwegians hate the Nazis.	German armies invade Belgium, Luxembourg, the Netherlands, and France. Many people begin to join the Resistance.

▲ By 1942 the Nazis had begun systematically rounding up Jews. An estimated six million Jews were killed during World War II, roughly four million of them in **death-camps**. This slaughter is known as the **Holocaust**.

Terrors of German occupation

- Starvation—the Nazis took most food for themselves.

- Curfew—people had to stay at home at night or risk being shot by the police.

- The Gestapo—the German security police could arrest anyone.

- Torture—many prisoners were tortured by the Gestapo.

- Travel problems—people could not even visit the next town without permission.

- Censorship—the Nazis controlled all media, including radio broadcasts and newspapers. Listening to Allied radio was a crime.

- Being spied on—collaborators "told tales" on their neighbors.

Eyewitness

Cornelia Fuykschot was twelve in May 1940 when the Netherlands was invaded. Her parents were listening in horror to the early morning radio news: "Parachutists have landed!" She remembered her father's grim voice say "This is war," while her mother calmly said "Let's have breakfast," knowing that life had to carry on, somehow. The Dutch people would not be free until 1945.

April 6, 1941

Yugoslavia and Greece are invaded by Germany. Partisans (resistance groups) fight back.

June 22, 1941

Germany invades the Soviet Union. Millions of Russians are killed.

January–May 1942

The Japanese conquer Malaya, Singapore, the Dutch East Indies, and the Philippines.

Resistance Fighters

Resistance groups in occupied countries such as France, the Netherlands, and the Philippines formed "underground" secret armies. Sometimes Resistance groups fought gun-battles with enemy troops, but more often they used **sabotage**—wrecking factory machines or blowing up railroad tracks.

Allied agents were trained in spying and secret warfare. They landed in occupied countries by parachute, plane, or submarine to help the Resistance. It was very dangerous. For example, anyone caught by the German security police, the Gestapo, faced almost certain death. The Japanese acted cruelly also. They killed anyone they suspected of helping the Filipino Resistance.

Eyewitness

Lise de Baissac was a French secret agent working for the British **Special Operations Executive (SOE)**. In September 1942, she parachuted into France, and rented an apartment in the town of Poitiers—next door to the Gestapo headquarters. "I was very lonely," she remembered, because "Having false [identity] papers, I never received a letter or a telephone call." She returned to England in 1943, but was back in France in April 1944, carrying guns and explosives for sabotage missions. Lise de Baissac survived the war and died in 2004.

▼ Men and women with jobs in factories, garages, schools, and stores risked their lives to work and fight for the Resistance.

14

Warsaw uprising

500,000 Polish Jews were prisoners in the Warsaw ghetto. Most were starving and sick. In 1942, the Nazis began removing 5,000 people a day. They took them to the gas chambers. In April 1943, 1,500 resistance fighters led by Mordechai Anielewicz fought the Nazis for three weeks. All but 80 Jews were killed in this Warsaw uprising. Anielewicz, along with others, killed himself rather than be captured.

▲ German soldiers in Warsaw, the center of Polish resistance to the Nazis. The Jewish uprising of 1943 was crushed. A Polish uprising in 1944 also failed.

Resistance tactics

- Each Resistance group had its own network of fighters and helpers.

- "Safe houses" were used as hiding places.

- Couriers rode bicycles from town to town with secret messages.

- Agents hid radios in suitcases or under floorboards.

- Resistance groups smuggled shot-down Allied airmen to safety.

▲ Members of the French Resistance study weapons dropped by parachute into Nazi-occupied France.

15

NATIONS HOLD ON

In countries at war, public services had to continue, despite damage to roads, railroads, and factories. Governments urged people to support the war effort.

Keeping on the move

People had to get to work every day and night, too. There was very little fuel because of gasoline rationing—in the United States, most people got only four, then later three, gallons per week. It was important to keep buses and trains moving. Railroads and shipping ports were vital to keep food and war supplies flowing.

In countries where there were air raids, city workers repaired broken water and gas pipes, and reconnected electric supplies. Firefighters fought blazes started by incendiary (fire) bombs. Rescuers dug out people trapped beneath collapsed buildings.

▲ Listening to the radio. Allied leaders Franklin D. Roosevelt and Winston Churchill spoke to their people on the radio. So did Hitler in Germany.

The media war

There was a **propaganda** war to encourage people to keep fighting and working for the war effort. Radio and newspapers spread war messages. Posters urged people to work harder, talk less, turn off lights, walk to work, and plant vegetables! In some countries, movie and stage theaters were closed at the start of the war, in case they were bombed. Later they were reopened because they were good for morale.

In Germany, Joseph Goebbels made sure that movies, radio, newspapers, and posters preached the Nazi view of the war. In the United States, people listened to popular radio programs such as Walter Winchell's fast-paced "Jergen's Journal," John D. Hughes' "News and Views," and Edward R. Murrow's "This … is London." Everyone could recognize these voices.

March 1940	Fall 1940	December 8, 1941
Professional soccer is re-started in Britain. Sports are good for public morale and crowds soon pack the soccer grounds.	Edward R. Murrow sends live radio reports to the United States, describing the Blitz on London. He tells how ordinary people are coping.	Broadcasting to Americans, President Roosevelt speaks of a "date which will live in infamy" after Japan attacks Pearl Harbor.

Typical wartime slogans:

We can't win without them
Poster encouraging women to work (USA)

Walk when you can
Poster urging people to walk whenever possible (Britain)

Blackout means black
Reminding people to shut curtains and blinds at night (USA)

Keep mum—the world has ears
Warning people not to gossip in case spies are listening (USA)

If THEY starve WE starve
Asking people to save food scraps for farm animals (Britain)

▲ Repair gangs worked constantly to keep Britain's railroads, water mains, telephone cables, and other essential services running through the Blitz.

Eyewitness

"Things got more difficult as the months went by. Water and gas got cut off due to bombed gas and water mains. Industry was disrupted with electricity cuts. Permanent waves [hair-curling using electric curlers] were a hazard ... a power-cut left you wet, cold, and with half a perm."

Leonora Pitt, from Walsall, England. She worked in an iron foundry with her grandfather, father, uncle, and brother.

March–April 1942

British bombers target the German port of Lübeck. In retaliation, German planes bomb historic British towns.

April 1942

Japan experiences a U.S. air raid for the first time. American B-25 bombers launched from an aircraft carrier attack Tokyo.

January 1944

German factories are hit hard by Allied bombing. The Nazis order all children over ten to do war work (such as clearing up bomb damage).

Digging for Victory

Governments sent out millions of brochures explaining how people on the home front could help to win the war. One way was to grow more food. In the United States, a government poster showed a tractor on a farm, leading tanks and airplanes. Its message, "Food Comes First," emphasized how important food was to the war effort. America's armed forces and its allies would need tons of supplies.

Gardening and the Land Army

Books and newspaper articles showed new gardeners how to prepare soil, plant seeds, and harvest crops. Short films featuring gardening tips were shown in movie theaters. Children's books taught kids how to grow plants.

More land was plowed to boost farm production. By the summer of 1942, more than six million American men had joined the armed forces or gone to work in war industries since 1940. At first, many women volunteered to help in the fields. Then, in 1943, the Women's Land Army was formed. It recruited women to work on farms and in forests. They worked long hours driving tractors, caring for animals, and harvesting crops.

▲ Posters like this one urged people to grow their own food. By 1944 roughly 18 million "victory gardens" were growing about 40 percent of the fresh vegetables eaten in the United States.

▶ In the United States and Britain, crops were planted in many unusual places. Cabbages were grown on top of air raid shelters. There were even vegetables in the dried-up moat of the Tower of London (pictured here).

Eyewitness

Britain also had a Women's Land Army. Its members were known as "land girls." Doreen Godfrey joined it at age 17, in 1941. In 1942, while out in the fields with a horse and cart feeding the cattle, she was shot at by a German plane. She was hit in the foot and had to wear a plaster cast for a year. Experienced land girls passed on tips to newcomers, such as how to repair leaky shoes with melted beeswax and castor oil.

▲ The Dig for Victory campaign was popular in the United States. Even children were encouraged to start "victory gardens."

◄ Women gathering wheat in southern England, 1944. Many "land girls" learned to drive tractors as well as handle horses.

The Women's Land Army

- There was a Women's Land Army (WLA) in World War I (1914–1918).

- It was re-formed in 1943.

- The WLA recruited more than one million women workers.

- Women laborers were paid between 25 and 40 cents per hour.

MAKE DO WITH LESS

People were urged not to waste food and precious materials. Slogans like "Make Do with Less" and "Use it up, wear it out, make it do or do without" told people not to throw away things that could be repaired or recycled.

Salvage = recycling

"Salvage" meant recycling. Children collected old pans and scrap metal because it could be used to make new planes and tanks. People handed in rubber boots, toys, tires, and even inflatable beach toys so the rubber could be reused. Meat bones were turned into glue and explosives. Waste paper was recycled and envelopes were reused.

Make your own clothes

By 1942, top fashion designers were making clothes that used less material. Many people made their own clothes: turning a blanket into a coat for instance. Women and children knitted wool hats, gloves, and scarves. Many U.S. families sent "clothes bundles" to Great Britain, where there were bigger shortages than in the United States.

Before the war, Britain had relied on ships to bring in much of its fuel, factory materials, and food (such as wheat). Now, however, German submarines were sinking hundreds of Allied ships crossing the Atlantic with supplies from the United States and other allies.

WPA

OCCUPIED TERRITORY

SALVAGE SCRAP TO BLAST THE JAP

THIRTEENTH NAVAL DISTRICT ★ UNITED STATES NAVY

▶ This U.S. poster urged Americans to salvage scrap metal in order to help their country's armed forces defeat the Japanese.

January 8, 1940	January 1942	February 1942
Food rationing begins in Britain. Everyone is given a ration book. In June 1941, clothes are also rationed.	Tires are rationed in the United States. The U.S. Army needs them for jeeps, tractors, and airplanes.	Australia rations food and clothes. Meat rationing, Australians are told, means more food for Britain.

Clothes in wartime

- Women's suits had shorter, slimmer skirts, and short jackets.

- Many fashions looked like working clothes. Women wore pants in public as well as for work.

- Shoes had heels of less than one inch.

- In Britain, all clothes were rationed. In 1943, a family got 48 points. A child's dress was 8 points and a woman's coat 15.

- In occupied countries, there were few new clothes to buy.

In the News

"Except for shoes—which are limited to three pairs a year for each person—clothes rationing is not in sight ... "

"The government is strict about the ban on pleasure driving ... "

"Candy is still plentiful ..."

From a report on the home front in the Stars and Stripes newspaper in June 1943. The Stars and Stripes was published for the American armed forces in Europe.

◄ In Britain, "utility clothes" were designed to look stylish. They had to be made cheaply from the scarce materials available.

March 1942

Germany suffers food shortages. By 1944, bread is severely rationed.

May 1942

Gasoline is rationed in the eastern United States, and nationwide by December. Coffee is rationed at the end of the year.

April 1943

Meat, lard, canned food, and cheese are rationed in the United States. Wages are frozen to keep prices steady.

Coping with Rationing

In 1942 the U.S. government began to ration some important goods, including food. Rationing made sure that basic foods were shared equally and not wasted. Cooks were encouraged to make the best use of foods that were plentiful. They tried recipes from books such as the *Good Housekeeping Cookbook* and *How to Cook a Wolf*. The government published pamphlets such as *Eat Well to Work Well* and *99 Ways to Share the Meat*.

MAKE DO WITH LESS

Coupons

The government controlled the sale of meat, eggs, sugar, and other foods. Families were given coupons for each type of food. A coupon allowed people to buy a certain amount of that food, if that food was available. Meat was scarce, for example, so people ate much more cottage cheese. Margarine took the place of real butter, and macaroni and cheese dinners were popular because they required just one coupon. Rationing meant that people ate less, but most kept healthy. They did not eat as much red meat and fat.

Food overseas

In some countries, many poorer children actually ate better because of rationing. There was much less food where there was fighting. In Russia, China, and in the Netherlands in 1944–1945, food shortages meant that many people starved.

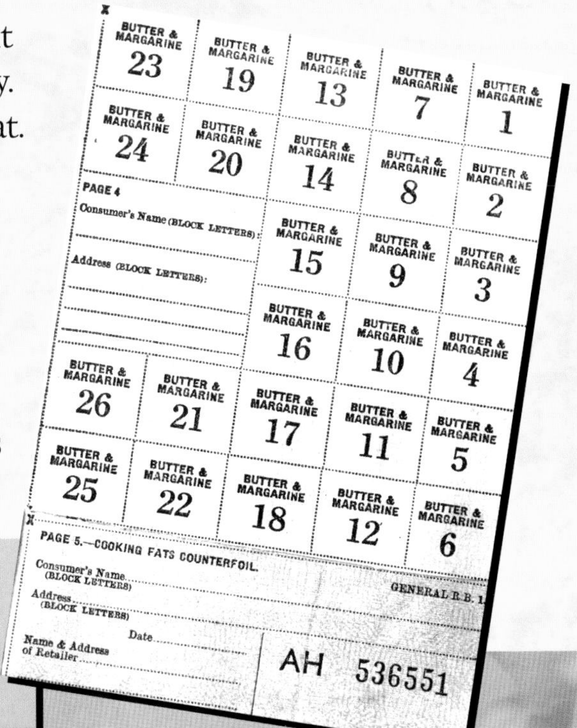

Wartime foods and recipes

Wartime meals included many unfamiliar foods and recipes:

- Food writer M.F.K. Fisher published a recipe for Tomato Soup Cake.

- Whale meat went on sale in Britain.

- German families made a sauce from beech nuts, salt, and an onion, to pour over potatoes.

- They also made "ersatz" (imitation) coffee from acorns.

A ration book page with numbered coupons labeled BUTTER & MARGARINE (23, 19, 13, 7, 1, 24, 20, 14, 8, 2, 15, 9, 3, 16, 10, 4, 26, 21, 17, 11, 5, 25, 22, 18, 12, 6). PAGE 4, Consumer's Name (BLOCK LETTERS), Address (BLOCK LETTERS). PAGE 5.—COOKING FATS COUNTERFOIL. Consumer's Name (BLOCK LETTERS), Address (BLOCK LETTERS), Date, Name & Address of Retailer. GENERAL R.B. 1. AH 536551

▶ Every person was given a ration book. You could buy only a limited amount of rationed foods per week.

▶ Children in Britain enjoyed food sent from the United States, such as cans of Spam and fresh eggs, supplied under the Lend-Lease program.

Eyewitness

William Anderson was just seven years old when the war ended. He remembered mealtimes:

"I realize how my mother and grandmother stretched items to the limit, such as mixing bread and onions with hamburger meat, then frying it. It was done, of course, to make the meat feed more people."

Most people had to eat less meat in wartime. Presents of food became popular, something we would find strange today.

◀ A wartime cook made do with whatever was in the stores or could be found locally. "Have you tried young stinging nettles boiled as a vegetable?" was one suggestion.

FAMILY LIFE

It was difficult to have a normal family life. Many families were separated by the war. Men and women were away in the armed forces or doing war work. Many who left home never returned.

Millions of people were in the services—the army, navy, and air force. For many, "joining up" soon meant going overseas to fight. At home, many women took full-time jobs, and this meant leaving the family for the first time. Before the war, grown-up sons and daughters had often lived at home until they got married. Now many were leaving home by the age of 18.

Eyewitness

"I was married in 1943. Everyone in the village helped ... people gave me lard, sugar, fruit, and eggs, and the baker made us a wedding cake. I wore a gray suit, white silk blouse, and navy blue hat and shoes ... bought with coupons saved up for over one year."

A war bride remembers her wedding in June 1943. Quoted in The Home Front *(1981).*

▶ Many couples married, in spite of rationing and dangers. Newlyweds were often separated, but hoped to build new lives together when peace came.

24

September 1939

Australia, Canada, and India join the war on Britain's side. Men and women from these countries enroll for war service.

October 1940

The United States calls up men for military service—the first peacetime compulsory draft in U.S. history.

January 1942

First U.S. soldiers arrive in the United Kingdom, in Northern Ireland. Soon, thousands of Americans are based in Britain, North Africa, and Australia.

Separations and new responsibilities

With so many men away, many children grew up without seeing much of their fathers. Servicemen came home only for brief rest periods or "leaves." People serving overseas were away for many months or years. Men who were captured by the enemy and held as prisoners of war were not seen by their families for many years. When families were reunited in 1945, children and parents had to get to know one another again.

In wartime, older children grew up fast. More of them had mothers who worked, and many children returned from school to an empty home. They helped clean the house and take care of younger brothers and sisters.

The worries of war

Wartime life was tiring and stressful. People spent hours on slow trips by train or bus and waited in long lines outside stores. Yet they had to work very hard. And every family dreaded the news that a relative or friend was wounded, missing, or killed in action.

In many countries, people did not get enough sleep due to the air raids. Families whose houses were bombed went to stay with relatives or friends. There was much upheaval and moving from place to place.

25

December 1942	Spring 1943	1944–1945
Sir William Beveridge announces plans for a "welfare state" with free schools and health care in Britain after the war.	All women in Britain aged 18–45 must register for part-time or full-time war work.	More than 15 million Americans are in the armed forces. Not until after May 1945 do Allied troops start to come home.

Keeping in Touch

During World War II, millions of people travelled far from home, often for the first time in their lives. Before the war, only the wealthy had travelled abroad for vacations.

Meeting the world

The Allied forces were huge and multi-national. Among the men and women in uniform were Americans, French, Poles, Australians, New Zealanders, Canadians, South Africans, British, Indians, West Indians, and many more. Many U.S. troops went to Britain. They were warned that wartime Britain was different than home. And most British people knew about the United States only from movies. Before 1942, few had met an American. They were surprised to learn that African-American soldiers did not serve in the same units as white soldiers in the U.S. Army.

The war brought new experiences and new friends, and strangers quickly became pals. Most Americans and British got along well and many friendships were made. Many wartime friendships endured for life.

In the News

"If you expect white cliffs and thatched cottages, you will be disappointed ... The people will be glad to see you but their enthusiasm is usually of a rather quiet sort."

Extract from a leaflet welcoming U.S. servicemen to Britain in 1942

▲ A wartime **telegram** was seldom good news. A brief official message usually told the reader that a relative was missing in action or dead.

Eyewitness

Some words in American English were not the same in British English, as Robert Arbid, an American soldier, discovered. The accent was very different, too:

"We were amazed to find that people [in England] used their own peculiar language ... new to our ears!"

Welcome letters

Letters, rather than phone calls, kept families in touch. Troops overseas waited expectantly for the next mail delivery, hoping for letters from wives, girlfriends, or parents. Birthday and holiday cards were smaller than in peacetime, but still treasured. So were family photos, perhaps showing a baby that an absent father had not yet seen.

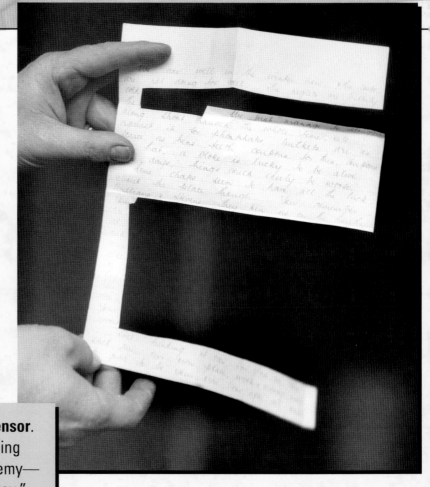

▶ Soldiers' letters were read by a **censor**. The censor crossed or cut out anything he or she thought might help the enemy— such as "I am leaving for Hawaii today," or "we have just been given new rifles."

◀ A U.S. soldier in 1945 said: "We have learned in the years of being away from home that mail from our families and friends is the thing that kept us going in spirit."

A CHANGED WORLD

In 1945, people in the Allied nations celebrated victory with parades and street parties. When the victory parties were over, the post-war world presented new challenges.

People remembered the friendship shared on the Home Front. They recalled funny moments, but seldom spoke about the fear, hardship, and sadness. The war was enormously costly. Nearly everyone had lost a friend or a relative. Across much of Europe and Asia, towns and villages were in ruins, industries were shattered, and roads, ports, and railroads were wrecked. There was a huge rebuilding task ahead.

Hopes for a new world

After six years of war, people were exhausted but looked forward to a brighter future. During the battle against bombs, shortages, and blackouts, they had hung on in the hope of victory and peace. Most of the **Allies** believed the war had been right, to defeat evil and make sure that nothing like the Holocaust would ever happen again. Germany and Japan were occupied by the Allies and faced years of reconstruction, but even in the defeated countries most people were relieved the war was over.

In 1945 millions of servicemen handed in their uniforms and weapons and returned to civilian life. As they planned for the future, people rebuilt their homes and picked up the pieces of family life. Some went back to their old jobs; others had fresh plans now that there was peace.

▶ People all over the world celebrated victory with street parties and parades. These revelers in New York are rejoicing on Victory in Europe Day (VE Day), May 8, 1945.

28

TIMELINE

1939

June 1 Women's Land Army is re-formed in Britain.
September 1 Germany invades Poland. World War II begins.
September 3 Britain and France declare war on Germany. Evacuation of children from British cities has already begun.

1940

January Food rationing begins in Britain.
April Germany invades Denmark and Norway.
May Germany invades Belgium, the Netherlands, and France.
June 30 Germany invades the Channel Islands.
June U.S. government tells all foreigners they must register with the Federal authorities because it is believed they might be a threat to security.
July Britain is threatened by a German invasion.
September The Blitz on British towns and cities begins. Women serve as air raid precaution (ARP) wardens, ambulance drivers, and voluntary helpers.
November 14 German planes bomb Coventry in Britain.

1941

March British government takes new powers to order people to do war work. People are asked not to use buses and trains after 4 p.m. so workers can get home.
April Germany and its allies invade Greece and Yugoslavia.
May Worst Blitz raids on London.
June Germany and its allies invade the Soviet Union.
June Clothes rationing begins in Britain.

July Coal is rationed in Britain.
December 7 Japanese attack on Pearl Harbor brings the United States into the war.
December 8 Britain and Canada declare war on Japan.

1942

January U.S. government puts Japanese-Americans in special camps because it fears they might help Japan in the war.
February Japanese forces move close to Australia. Australia's prime minister, John Curtin, announces food rationing.
March Introduction of utility clothing in Britain.
May Start of gasoline rationing in the United States.
June Last Jewish schools in Germany are closed by the Nazis.
July Candy is rationed in Britain.
October U.S. government "freezes" wages, rents, and prices.

1943

February Allies begin bombing Germany night and day.
February A German army surrenders at Stalingrad, ending German advance into the Soviet Union.
April-May Some foods, including meat and sugar, are rationed in the United States. Around this time, all women in Britain aged 18–45 must register for war work.
May The Warsaw Rising of Polish resistance fighters is crushed.
July Allies land in Sicily to begin the invasion of Italy.

1944

April Very heavy Allied air attacks on German cities.

April Much of southern England is a huge military camp, in preparation for the invasion of Europe.
June 6 D-Day; Allied armies invade France to begin the liberation of France.
June 13 First German V-1 flying bomb falls on London.
July In the United States, more than 3,000 childcare centers are providing care for an estimated 125,000 pre-school children of war workers.
September Streetlights turned on in Britain as the blackout is eased at the end of the Blitz. V-2 attacks begin.
September Allies enter Germany. Nazis form their own "Home Guard" called the *Volkssturm*.
October German bread ration is cut to one loaf per week.

1945

February 14 Allied bombers destroy Dresden in Germany.
April 12 Death of U.S. President F. D. Roosevelt. Harry S Truman becomes president.
April 30 Hitler kills himself as Soviet armies close in on Berlin.
May 2 Berlin is captured by Soviet armies.
May 7 Germany surrenders.
May 8 VE (Victory in Europe) Day. End of the war in Europe.
August 6 Allies drop an atomic bomb on Japanese city of Hiroshima and another on Nagasaki three days later. Japan surrenders.
August 14 V-J Day (Victory over Japan) ends the war.

GLOSSARY

air raid attack on a target by airplanes dropping bombs

Allies nations that fought against Germany, Japan, and Italy during World War II

blackout measures to reduce all visible lights at night to hide possible targets from enemy bombers

Blitz short for *Blitzkrieg*, German for "lightning war." The term "Blitz" is used to describe the German bombing of Britain that began in 1940.

casualties people injured or killed during a war

censor official who read letters and newspaper articles to remove any information useful to an enemy

civilian someone who is not in the armed forces

collaborator person who cooperates with an enemy that has taken over his or her country

death-camps Nazi prison camps in which Jews and other people were killed, sometimes in gas chambers

evacuate move people from danger to safer places

ghetto area of a city within which Jews were confined

Holocaust mass killing of Jews and others by the Nazis during World War II

identity papers papers showing a person's photo and personal details

Nazi member of the National Socialist German Workers' Party, led by Adolf Hitler

occupation when a country is invaded and ruled by another country

patriotic loving and supporting one's own country

propaganda control of information in the media to show your own side in a good light

Resistance groups of people who fought against enemy forces occupying their country

sabotage break equipment or slow down work in a factory, or damage railroad tracks, bridges, and telephone wires to hinder an enemy

sandbags bags filled with dirt or sand to protect buildings and people from bomb damage

Special Operations Executive (SOE) British organization that sent secret agents to help the Resistance in France and other occupied countries

telegram message sent by phone lines for speed, but delivered as a short printed message

war bond piece of paper bought from the government. It could be sold back several years later, for more money than was paid for it.

FINDING OUT MORE

If you are interested in finding out more about World War II, here are some more books you might find useful.

Further reading

Your local public library's adult section should have plenty of war books, including books about what it was like to live on the home front. Written by people who were actually there, such books will give you an idea of what ordinary people thought about the war and their part in it.

Books for younger readers

Adams, Simon. *World War II*. New York: DK Children, 2004.

Ambrose, Stephen E. *The Good Fight*. New York: Simon & Schuster, 2001.

Colman, Penny. *Rosie the Riveter: Women Working on the Homefront in World War II*. New York: Knopf 1995.

Dolan, Edward F. *America in WWII – 1943*. Brookfield: Millbrook, 1992.

Josephson, Judith Pinkerton. *Growing Up in World War II: 1941–1945*. Minneapolis: Lerner, 2002.

King, David C. *World War II Days*. New York: Wiley, 2000.

Kuhn, Betsy. *Angels of Mercy: The Army Nurses of World War II*. Illinois: Atheneum, 1999.

Panchyk, Richard. *WWII for Kids*. Chicago: Chicago Review Press, 2002.

Tanaka, Shelley. *Attack on Pearl Harbor*. New York: Hyperion, 2001.

Also the Heinemann Library *Holocaust* and *Witness to History* series (several titles).

INDEX

air raid shelters 10

air raids 7, 9, 11, 16

Allies 4–5, 24, 26, 28

baseball 9

Battle of Britain 8

black market 22

blackout 17

Blitz 4, 9, 11, 17, 25

Blitzkrieg 4

bombing 4–5, 7–9, 11, 17

candy 21

casualties 4–5

censorship 13, 27

children 7, 9–11, 19, 22, 25

Churchill, Winston 16

civilian deaths 4–5

Civilian Public Service 9

clothes 20–21

collaborators 12–13

concentration camps 10, 12

conscientious objectors 9

cooking and recipes 22–23

curfew 13

daily life 8, 25

death-camps 13

Dig for Victory 10, 18–19

draft (call-up) 6

entertainment 16

Europe, occupied 12–13

evacuation 7, 11, 25

factories 8

family life 24–25

firefighters 16

food supplies 6, 9–10, 18–20, 22–23

France 5, 8, 12, 14

French Resistance 14–15

friendships 26

gas masks 6, 10

Germany 4–7, 9, 12–13, 16–17, 20, 23, 28

Gestapo 13–14

ghettos 12, 15

GIs 24, 26

Hitler, Adolf 5–6, 16

Holocaust 13, 28

Hughes, John D. 16

identity papers 12

incendiary bombs 16

Japan 5, 7, 12–13, 17, 28

Jewish people 10, 12–13, 15

"joining up" 24

land girls 19

Lend-Lease program 23

letters and telegrams 11, 26–27

London 5, 18

Make Do with Less 20–21

munitions factories 8

Murrow, Edward R. 16

Nazis 6, 12–13, 15–16

Netherlands 13–14, 22

Norway 12

occupation 4, 12–13

patriotism 9

Pearl Harbor 4–5, 7, 16

Philippines 4, 12, 13, 14

poison-gas bombs 6

Poland 4, 12, 15

prisoners of war 25

propaganda 16

public services 16–17

radio 16, 18

rationing 9, 16, 20–23

recycling 10, 20

resistance groups 12–15

Roosevelt, Franklin D. 9, 16

sabotage 14

salvage 20

sandbags 7

schools 9–11

shelter-trenches 7

sirens 10

Special Operations Executive (SOE) 14

sports 16

transportation 16–17

VE Day 28

war bonds 10

war effort 8–11, 16

war work 8–9, 17, 25

Warsaw risings 15

weddings 24

welfare state 25

Winchell, Walter 16

women 8–9, 25

Women's Land Army (WLA) 18–19